AF571811

TOTAL THANKS

TOTAL THANKS

CONSTANCE P. THARP

foreword by
Louis B. Tharp, Ph.D.

LOGOS INTERNATIONAL Plainfield, New Jersey

Unless otherwise indicated, all Scripture quotations are taken from the Revised Standard Version.

Total Thanks
Copyright ©1978 by Logos International
All rights reserved
Printed in the United States of America
International Standard Book Number: 0-88270-267-X
Library of Congress Catalog Card Number: 78-51963
Logos International, Plainfield, N.J. 07061

A personal book of the experiences of

Sharon Coursey
____

in whose life God's love and care has been manifested.

CONTENTS

Suggestions on How to Use This Book

I am not the author of this book. *You* are. You may find some of my suggested thoughts to be useful, for which I will be glad, but this is *your* book to express *your* thankfulness for God's work in *your* life. Even if no one ever reads it other than you, you can be sure that the Lord reads over your shoulder at every line. Ironically, even though there are some four billion people on His earth—each of whom is indebted to Him for their every breath of life—very few of them will ever sit down and write such a "thank you" to Him. I think He's going to be pleased as punch to read yours.

You may decide to pass the finished book along as a written testimony of God's good gifts to you. Someone may have given you the book, in fact, for that very purpose. It could be considered rather flattering that someone—a son or daughter, or your spouse perhaps—wants to know what God has done in your life.

There is a much more serious purpose, however, intended in writing such a spiritual autobiography. Such a book may be used by someone as a source of strength and encouragement long after God has taken you to be with Him. It can remain as a testimony of your own *personal* relationship with God which might greatly influence a child or grandchild, or even great-grandchild, who perhaps never knew you personally.

Only God knows how such a book may be used by others. You are going to find out, however, how He uses it for *you*. He alone can really show you how to best use this book. In the meantime, here are some of my suggestions.

1. Ask God to help you write it.
2. Remember that you are thanking God. It's very easy to begin writing about your *own* "spiritual success story." You may find yourself doing just that. That's okay, because if you sincerely did ask God to help you, then He will eventually draw that to your attention. Then you can have one more thing for which to thank Him!
3. Don't write "for effect." Even if you plan to let others someday read the record of God's work with you, don't write with other people in mind. As a testimony, nothing is less effective than a "contrived story" told "for evangelistic effect." Nothing is more attractive to believers and unbelievers alike than *sincerity*. And people can tell the difference.
4. Learn as you go. Don't try to rush through the book, filling up every page, as though it's dishonoring to God to not have something to thank Him for in every area of life. "For everything there is a season, and a time for every matter under heaven" (Eccles. 3:1). God works His miracles in our lives with exact timing. Relax. He'll fill in every part of *you* completely.

And as that happens, you can fill in every part of the book completely. Then you are going to need a new book, because you will find out that the "you" that you thought was a completed "house" was only the first floor of the RCA Building.
5. Be honest.

Somehow, maybe because we ourselves are so limited in understanding ourselves and other people, it is very easy to think of God in the same way. We confess something to Him very often with the notion that it must come as a great big surprise, as if He didn't know all about it already.

So if you find yourself sincerely doubting whether you have *anything* to be thankful for at some point in your life, don't put this book on a shelf until you can "get spiritual enough again" to start writing "acceptable" things to God. Get your book off the shelf and start writing. If you are doubtful now, think how much more convinced of God's faithfulness you are going to be later, when you see the way He worked *even through your doubts*. Unless you are honest—writing your doubts and defeats as well as your faith and victories—you won't have the kind of *real life* experience book which can stand the test of trial and discouragement. You'll have a "half book"—great to read on those sunshine days when everything is *obviously* going well, but not much help at all when the skies look grey or stormy.

In case you still think God is bothered by "whole books"—in which people write their failures and doubts as well as their successes and faith—just start reading the Book of Psalms. David was a man after God's own heart (1 Sam. 13:14) because he was totally honest with God, and had *real* fellowship with Him. He and God had heart-to-heart—honest emotion to honest emotion—conversation. Best of all David didn't "shelve himself" when he sinned. Both an adulterer and a murderer, David still came back to talk to God, and to praise Him even more fully (2 Sam. 11:2-12:10; Ps. 51).

6. Read back over your *Total Thanks* book every now and then, just to remind yourself of God's goodness. It may also dumbfound you to recall how you have grown up in the faith. Jesus says that we will each grow as we let ourselves become a part of His vine (John 15:4-5). At another time He describes our faith as beginning as a tiny mustard seed but becoming a huge tree (Matt. 13:31-32). Vines and mustard seeds grow slowly, and it is easy for the impatient branches to think they are stunted. But reading back over your own spiritual experiences several months or years later, it's a happy, and often jarring, experience to

compare what was a thin and shaky plant to what has become a strong and stable tree.

7. Don't forget to read the Bible. From cover to cover it is a book about gratitude. Each individual book is the historical experience of God's work with His people and their thankful reply to Him—or their failure to be thankful. Each of the four gospel writers tell about the marvelous things Jesus did and said for the people around Him, and for us all. The Book of Acts is a record of God's work with His young church, written to proclaim the greatness of God's faithfulness to His people. Its goal is to prepare us for that day when we shall see for ourselves what John saw in his Revelation:

> And I heard every creature in heaven and on earth and under the earth and in the sea, and all therein, saying, "To him who sits upon the throne and to the Lamb be blessing and honor and glory and might for ever and ever!" (5:13)

Foreword

THE THEOLOGY AND PSYCHOLOGY OF THANKFULNESS

When Connie told me of her idea for the *Total Thanks* book, I promised her I'd write a theological preface to it. As I began casually to research the topic of thankfulness, my "assignment" slowly became one of the most fascinating intellectual and emotional journeys I have experienced.

Thankfulness has never been one of my own shining qualities. My mother has sometimes remarked that she wishes she had taught me how to say "please" and "thank you." Actually, she did teach me those things—very well, in fact. But because they were, to me, only ritualistic manners, I rebelliously resisted the frequent use of such words while I was still a teenager. I always admired people who did say the appropriate polite phrases of gratitude, but it seemed somehow phony for me to do it.

The same process occurred later when I became a member of the Christian church. My faith was so real to me, so emotional and personal, that I could not understand how others could "casually" (it seemed to me) utter words so meaningful that *I* couldn't say them without deep emotion. I also became aware of some subtle psychological pressures to conform to this "spiritualized language" to prove the reality of one's Christian faith.

Once again, I resisted such ritualistic conformity, making it a point to avoid such religious terminology. I still do. For me, personally, to use a special vocabulary when talking about God or to God would seem very artificial—even phony. Again, that's just me. I envy those who freely and genuinely express themselves this way.

I am describing my own personal experience for two

reasons. First of all, I want to be honest and up-front about my own discomfort with the frequent use of "pious phrases." Perhaps others who have had similar feelings will be glad to meet at least one other member of the church who shouts his own gratitude usually within the silence of his own soul. Second, I want to say, from my own personal experience, that being thankful to God and to other people is, theologically and psychologically, crucial to living a fully abundant life.

The Theology of Thankfulness

If there's one theological truth that is probably beyond dispute, it is the axiom that God is perfect. He does not lack any good quality. He is "all-in-all," "unity," "one," "pure being"—all these words describe the One who is "self-sufficient"—the "uncreated."

This truth has a very remarkable consequence for us as creatures. It means that God has no needs. He doesn't need our gifts; He doesn't need our sacrifices. He doesn't even need our *thanks*. We are *free*! God's attitude toward us is the same—love—no matter what our attitude or response is.

That presents us with the uniquely human possibility: the choice to *spontaneously* respond to Him in thankfulness. How could thanks be genuine if it were coerced, or required? Genuine thanks is freely given. It is not a piece of good behavior by which we earn God's approval. God does not love us because we are thankful, but, rather, we are thankful because He has loved us. God's love pulls us along toward thankfulness. Our thankfulness cannot pull even one ounce more love out of Him.

God is the great giver, the great lover. There is

nothing which delights Him more than having His gifts received and appreciated. Our only "job" is the work of faith—to believe, to receive. Faith is an expression of the willingness to receive God's love—His gifts—and thankfulness is the emotional reaction to faith. On God's part there is the offer of love—given, unmerited grace. On our part, there is the decision of faith—an active choice to believe in God's love toward us and to receive it. And thankfulness is the emotional response we have to that decision.

It's so simple. Someone offers you a gift, you decide to take it, and the natural reaction is to thank them for it. Thankfulness rewards the giver, but it benefits the receiver even more. To receive without being thankful is to miss the joy of appreciation which is the real gift. A gift unappreciated is, in one sense, still ungiven.

Psychological Aspects of Thankfulness

Now we can see a parallel psychological principle involved here as well. We are only made happy by what we are thankful for. Whether it be material possessions, successes, friendships, love relationships—every factor which might bring us greater happiness only makes us actually happier as we appreciate it.

Let me give a personal example. Just this afternoon we took our trusty Chevrolet Blazer four-wheeling over the Silverado Canyon Road—"fun-trucking" as the TV advertisement calls it. I'm really in love with this machine. It has almost every off-road extra—padded roll bar, oversized tires, Jackman spoke wheels, Cibie quartz lights—the works. But it also has, as I discovered earlier this week, a bad U-joint, which creates a noticeable shake and rumble. As I drove along I found myself concentrating on this vibration, frowning as I projected the future expense, when suddenly I realized how I had fallen prey to the most common human pathology. I was being unthankful. Everything else in that car was functioning beautifully. The air conditioning was blowing cool air in my face while the temperature outside was over ninety degrees. The automatic transmission was smoothly shifting. The engine hadn't missed a beat. Probably one thousand parts—bearings, gears, rods, valves, pistons—all doing their job, and I am unthankfully critical of *one* U-joint. (The Blazer has four.)

It is easy to concentrate on the negative. So many of our daily 1,440 minutes are spent thinking about what is going wrong in life—business problems, disagreements, one burnt dish, a bad U-joint—that we usually waste much of our energy on feeling unhappy or worried about the 20 per cent trouble-areas of life. How much time do we spend feeling happy—*thankful*—for what is going right, the 80 per cent taken-for-granted areas?

Before you answer that question, here's a more difficult one. If God doesn't need our thankfulness, why does He encourage us throughout the Bible to be thankful? I think the answer is simple: *we* need it. It does us good to be thankful. In one sense, being thankful is the only thing we ever do that does us any good.

Human psychology is such that we are not made happy by what we acquire, whether it be material objects, personal relationships, or experiences, but by what we appreciate. In other words, the degree to which we are thankful—appreciative—determines our happiness in every area of life.

Let me give an illustration—a materialistic one. When we acquire something brand new—a new car, a house, a new sofa, even a new suit or dress—we are often keenly appreciative. We may even "fall in love" with that thing—but only for a short period of time. The same object six months later no longer so well appreciated brings us not even one-tenth of the excitement and happiness it gave to us originally. Our thankfulness is gone, and when it goes, boredom starts to set in. Not only boredom. Much more serious consequences occur when we lose our thankfulness.

Theologically, there is a sense in which thanklessness can be seen as the source of all sin. The temptation of Eve in the garden of Eden involved getting her to doubt whether God should be thanked—or blamed. The subtle serpent got Eve to forget that God had given her everything she needed and to concern herself with the one forbidden tree (Gen. 3:1-6). Next he questioned God's motives: "For God knows that when you eat of it your eyes will be opened, and you will be like God. . . ." Eve then made the free choice which resulted in the Fall—the decision to ignore what had been given to her and concentrate on her one supposed lack—a decision, by the way, which is also the classic choice involved in neurosis. The neurotic is usually obsessed with what he feels he lacks, rather than the positive factors of his life. Thankfulness is the bottom line source of mankind's original sin and of his everyday sins as well.

The Apostle Paul comes to the same analytical conclusion in his letter to all Christians in Rome: "So they are without excuse; for although they knew God they did not honor him as God *or give thanks to him* . . ." (1:20-21 italics mine).

One of the basic sins of mankind, theologically, is thanklessness. The antidote is faith—a joyful thanks to God for His love for us, shown to us by Jesus Christ. Psychologically, in personal relationships, the same principle holds true. Thanklessness is the major destructive force in human relationships. "Love makes the world go 'round," the song tells us. That's only half true. It's love that starts our world going 'round, but it's thankfulness that keeps our heads spinning. The most wildly spinning romance will eventually slow down and grind to a stop if there is not a day by day thankfulness expressed in smiles, kisses, and kind words of appreciation.

Keeping in Touch with Reality

It's sad but ironic that in most relationships we seldom realize how little we have appreciated a loved one until it is too late. Death or divorce often snaps us dramatically into touch with reality, and we realize the many personal little things we have taken for granted.

Psychologically, thankfulness is the perfect antidote for mental illness. Being thankful for all the good that we have going for us, rather than just the evil going against us, helps us keep our minds "balanced." Thankful strokes given to others usually result in thankful strokes returned to us. Nothing will keep a marriage alive longer than simple appreciation.

On a larger spectrum, theologically, being thankful to our Creator puts us into contact with ultimate reality. God did create; He sustains all life, and being thankfully aware of that fact keeps us in touch with physical as well as spiritual reality. To believe, or act as though we believe, that we ourselves are the source of life is to fly in the face of the most primal level of reality.

The world at large—now four billion persons—certainly gives God less than one percent of the thanks He is, in cold reality, due. While applauding themselves for such feats as the harnessing of the atom and missions to the moon, they seldom stop to consider the Maker of all atoms whose universe spans seventy billion light years.

Thankfulness for every breath we breathe, every morning we awake to a new day, even every heartbeat is not excessive sentimentality. It is in reality simply an awareness of the fragile fabric of our physical bodies in which a single malignant cell or tiny blood clot can end forever our common casually unthankful attitude.

It's not just the secular world which takes God for granted. Jesus said, "Not every one who says to me, 'Lord, Lord,' shall enter the kingdom of heaven. . ." (Matt. 7:21). The same holds true of thankfulness. Not everyone who says "thank you" to God is truly being thankful. The best illustration of this is the parable Jesus told of the Pharisee and the publican (Luke 18:9-14). The Pharisee begins his self-righteous prayer with the words, "God, I thank thee." But his attitude is ungrateful: ". . . that I am not like the other men. . . . I fast twice a week, I give tithes. . . ." Note that the worldly publican is not able to offer any words of thanks. In fact, he cannot even lift his head to pray. But the fact that he mutters, "God, be merciful to me a sinner!" evidences a humble faith in God's goodness—an indirect form of thankfulness. Jesus says of him that he "went down to his house justified."

It's easy to get trapped in words, to use the language of thankfulness without the feelings that should go with it. Part of the reason for this book is to encourage you to "spell out"—to specify in detail—those things for which you are indeed thankful.

Repeating catchy phrases is not "praising the Lord" unless sincere feeling goes along with the words.

More than anything else, we want to stress the importance of emotional honesty in completing your *Total*

Thanks book. It would be far better, like the publican, to write only one short but sincerely felt sentence than to fill the book with meaningless cliches or half-felt comments.

As a psychologist, I know the importance of emotional honesty—saying what you mean, not pretending to be more than you are, being yourself. I'm sure the Creator has not been suddenly enlightened by these insights from "modern" psychology. He's been promising for over twenty centuries that if "you will know the truth, . . . the truth will make you free" (John 8:32). Don't be afraid of truth then. Write what is truly within your heart because God knows it already, and He delights in having an absolutely honest relationship. Once you discover that, it will free you to be just *yourself*—and you'll be very, very thankful.

Louis B. Tharp, Ph.D.

TOTAL THANKS

Thanks to God for **little things**

Sometimes it's the little things in life that count. God has every hair on our heads numbered, so He's not about to just overlook the little details when He sends us His life valentines. Maybe you think that it's too much bother to God for you to ask him about such "small" problems. Try Him out and see! As you do, keep a record of those times when He has shown himself faithful in the little things in life. He doesn't forget us, so let's not forget that He remembered.

appt. situation
gas situation
work - attitude
writing class

Thanks to God for **the biggest thing of all—his creation**

"When I look at thy heavens, the work of thy fingers, the moon and the stars which thou hast established; what is man that thou art mindful of him . . ." (Ps. 8:3-4). In these few words the Psalmist has expressed poetically the twofold miracle of creation. The first miracle, the creation of a universe so immense that it absolutely staggers any man's imagination, makes every other miracle seem to be simply casual work for the hands of such a Maker. But the second, and perhaps most important part of the miracle is that this immense universe was designed and planned for man. What an undertaking—what a project—and what love behind it all! One scientist has estimated that, traveling at the speed of light (186,000 miles per second), it would require seventy billion years to traverse the universe—if indeed it can be traversed. In a single galaxy there may be as many as one hundred million stars, and—sit down before you read this—scientists estimate that there are billions of galaxies! And yet the Creator of all of this is so interested in each one of us on this speck of dust called earth that He has the hairs of our heads numbered. No wonder the biblical writers say so often "all power and all glory under heaven and earth is Thine."

Perhaps because it is the most obvious, the most "taken for granted" fact of life—the creation and the universe that now surrounds us—that we so seldom truly appreciate it. If this is all too true of you yourself then maybe it is time to open your eyes and look around at the wondrous things that God has wrought. Ask Him and He will teach you of His wonders day by day. Perhaps camping out under a canopy of stars, maybe through the pages of a book of science, at a first snowfall or a first flower in the spring—in hundreds of unique and individual ways—He will teach you personally to appreciate what He has done. As He does in each of these moments, write them in this book—a paragraph, perhaps later a single sentence, your own personal record of thankfulness to God for His universe.

Thanks to God for **my salvation**

God never brings two people to Himself in exactly the same way. Salvation is always personal, because God is personal. Not only did He provide the means of salvation by appearing in Person—the meek and lowly Jesus of the little town of Nazareth—but He brings each one of us to that salvation in a very personal way. Write in the following pages the unique story of how He first opened your eyes to see His Way and the Truth.

Thanks to God for **making it possible to love myself**

My husband, a psychologist, tells me that the biggest psychological problem of almost every client he meets is the lack of self-love. Inferiority feelings, guilt, doubts of the self in little areas and in big ones, this is a plague that has infected us all. Self-hate was the very first result of Adam's sin. From the very moment that Adam and Eve ate of the forbidden fruit they began to feel ashamed of themselves, ashamed of their own bodies, and most important even ashamed to converse or be seen by their own Maker *and Friend*. The doctrine of "original sin" has become rather unpopular in "modern" times. Ironically, however, the very same people who laughed at the idea of an original universal cause of self-hate nevertheless are agreed upon the universality of its effect. "Modern" psychology has finally caught up with the Bible in one area at least—they now see the root of our problem as a continual self-doubt.

Eve and her husband had good reason to be ashamed, for they had betrayed the trust of the One who had loved them, and had given them everything. Like so many of us they could not feel comfortable with themselves *as they were*, but had to seek that one extra fruit that they thought they needed to feel comfortable with themselves. Every time we ourselves feel that same feeling of inadequacy we are testifying that we are indeed Adam's children. Most of the time even while we are reading books about self-love, or trying desperately to gain it in some way, we are at that very time most involved in that feeling of incompleteness. There is no way for man to by some bootstrap method pull himself up to self-acceptance. The way to self-acceptance is not up, but down. The Apostle James says, "Humble yourselves before the Lord and he will exalt you" (James 4:10). Only God has made it possible for us to love ourselves and the only way He has made for that to happen is the way of the cross. Not merely the cross of the initial salvation but the daily cross of everyday humility. As Paul found out, God's strength is made perfect in our weakness (2 Cor. 12:9).

In the pages that follow describe those daily events by which God has taught you to relax with Him, and through that to relax with yourself. Thank Him for making it possible that you no longer have to be concerned about guilt, failure, insecurity, inadequacy, because you have a Friend who *likes you as you are.*

Thanks to God for **childhood memories**

Have you ever wondered what the world would be like if we all started out as adults? Jesus said of children, "to such belongs the kingdom of God" (Mark 10:14, Luke 18:16). Every one of us, then, has had a taste of heaven—in a way—during the innocence of our childhood. And even if the adults around us produced a hellish home environment, we ourselves—for a short time at least—have experienced being genuine, honest and without guile. Many have beautiful memories of our childhood, while others have only a few. But regardless of the number, the value of those precious moments of beauty, freedom, and childhood wonder are something to thank God for. In the following pages write those memories for which you are most thankful.

Thanks to God for **parents who loved me— imperfectly**

The commandment to "honor your father and mother" has a promise attached to it: "that your days may be long in the land" (Exod. 20:12). There are the obvious dangers of disobeying parents—the child who plays in the street, for instance, may shorten his days upon the earth. But anxiety shortens our days more commonly than trucks. It increases the cholesterol level of the blood, for one thing, which often has more deadly effect on the length of our days.

So often Christian young people whose parents do not know Jesus try to get them to "become saved"—often leading them to be further alienated. The young Christian would have done so much better to think about what his parents *have done* which have shown their love.

That's *honoring* them—honoring the gift of *life* and the gifts of love which they *have* given—instead of blaming them for *not* giving you what only God can give anyway—a knowledge and awareness of Him. In the following pages, remember and write down the ways in which your parents have shown their love to you.

Thanks to God for **a mate to share life with**

I once heard an old Baptist minister say, "A happy home is as close as we can get to heaven here on earth." I suppose he ought to have known, for he and his "bride" of thirty-eight years manifested that happiness in their own brightly lit faces. Marriage was God's first personal gift to man, for He saw that it was "not good for man to be alone." This is not to say that there are not those who have willingly chosen to remain single in order to serve the Lord in some special task. But most of us have been blessed with that very personal gift of a mate.

Just as God chose Eve and molded her to be the perfect wife for Adam, so also does He choose each one of us a mate with the same care for a perfect match. "You must be kidding!" you may find yourself saying at this point. But don't forget about the molding process! God often chooses two people whose differences will sandpaper each other into a perfect fit, though it may take a few years to smooth over the rough edges.

In the next few pages write the story of your own romance and marriage. Can you see the tracing of God's work in bringing the two of you together? What have you added to, and subtracted from, each other? Perhaps a good one-hour exercise would be to imagine your life without your mate. What would it be like had you been all alone? What lessons have you learned together that could never have been learned in isolation? Don't forget to thank God for the entire process because marriage was His idea from the beginning.

Thanks to God for **the miracles called children**

If God has brought into your life one of His little miracles—or maybe *several* miracles—then you know already the joy of watching one of these "little ones" grow. Think what life would be without them. (Maybe there are some days, however, in which such a thought is a pleasant momentary distraction!) Seriously though, few of the gifts God gives to us can bring such joy as do our children.

I'm not going to say any more here because in case you are one of those with several to write about you'll need all the space you can get. Tell the story of each of your children and the joy that they have brought uniquely and individually to your own life.

Thanks to God for **friends**

Acquaintances are many in life's way, but true friends are few. Loneliness is perhaps the most difficult of all burdens, perhaps for no other reason than because there is no one with whom to share it. Many times we forget to thank our friends for just being that—a friend. Sometimes we forget ourselves the significance and value that individual friendships bring to our lives. Imagine for a moment that you had none, not a single friend—and couldn't find one. Maybe through this fantasy—or perhaps a reality—you can begin to appreciate the value of friendship. On many occasions you can see clearly that it was God Himself who introduced two friends to each other. These friendships are very special, but even those which are formed through "natural" means have Him as their source—because it was He who originally said, "It is not good that the man should be alone" (Gen. 2:18). It is His purpose that we have many friends. In the following pages tell what God has done for you in the area of friendship.

Thanks to God for **daily bread**

Probably the "thing" for which God is most often thanked is food. Sometimes, however, our dinnertime blessings become stale, even though God's bread is every day fresh.

Write on these pages about those experiences in which you experience God's gift of daily bread in an uncommon way. How has He taught you to *really* be thankful for daily provisions on a level that was no longer in any way simply a "ritual"?

Thanks to God for **a healthy body**

Some people who have experienced severe sickness may find it a little difficult to write on this page without feeling hypocritical. If you are one of those who has suffered illness and pain, perhaps it might help to begin with a list of potential illnesses that you *don't* have. I'm not trying to underestimate the reality of pain or sickness, but sometimes it's easy to forget that though we may have one or two or even ten various ailments at the same time, there are several thousand possible ailments which could be afflicting our body in areas where it is still healthy. Very seriously, consider the possible things that can go wrong with the human body; there are literally thousands. And yet for the vast majority of us we continue on month after month, year after year with only a few of these "breakdowns." Most of us, in fact, will likely die from one *single* disease. My husband tells me that estimates of the percentage of illnesses which are basically psychosomatic range from 40 to 75 per cent. Maybe part of the reason for this high percentage of "self-inflicted" illnesses is the fact that most of us concentrate on our sicknesses rather than on our many areas of health. God must hear at least one hundred prayers concerning sickness for every one He hears thanking Him for the health that He has given us.

Once again I do not want to say that illness is unimportant and that we should not grieve for pain and suffering. But let's also be joyful for health in every area in which we find it. Start with your toes and work to the top of your head and begin to count the many ways in which your body is remarkably healthy and write your own medical report to God to thank Him for the many healthy parts of your body.

Thanks to God for **my eyes**

Before you write a single line on this subject, may I suggest that you spend at least one hour blindfolded. If it is safe, you might try walking around the house fumbling your way here and there in your own known environment. The world outside will be largely closed to you. You won't be able to drive a car and wherever people do take you, you will only hear and feel but never see again. Spend most of your time thinking about what it would be like to lose your sight now, or what it would be like had you never had the ability to see from birth. You would not know the difference between the colors. You would never see a sunset, or a loved one's face, or even your own face. Sit and imagine that you have never seen a tree or a flower or a window pane—the miracle of seeing through glass would be astounding! Imagine that you have never experienced seeing light. You have never seen the sky above or the earth beneath your feet or the trees and buildings which are in between. You have never seen the many, many objects which surround you within the home—a clock which you only hear ticking, a fire in the fireplace, the beautiful colors of food on the table. I could go on and on, and I hope *you* do just that!

Then when you fully learn what it means to be blind, take off the blindfold and begin to thank God for what you can see. You might want to write about the experience—or any other experiences that God gives to you along life's way—on these pages on which you can give thanks to God for your eyes.

Thanks to God for
the sense of hearing

You might want to learn appreciation for your ears through an experiment similar to the one I suggested for your eyes, this time plugging your ears to eliminate all sounds. Very possibly it will take a longer period of time to really begin to appreciate what you are missing in not being able to hear. The most obvious things will be conversation and perhaps the sound of the television set. But as time goes on you will begin to realize that there are much more serious problems confronting you. You will find yourself unable to use the telephone, unable to hear the doorbell, unable to hear a baby or child crying; soon you will find yourself very aware that the sense of hearing is a valuable one indeed.

Something of which most of us are not aware, however, is the marvelous ability of our ears to detect nuances of difference in sound. Imagine how it would be were we not able to hear the variation in notes, for instance, in music. Isn't it beautiful that we can tell direction and distance by sound as well? Begin to listen for every possible vibration which your God-given ears are able to translate into meaningful sound.

Some may point out that God has given an even keener sense of hearing to many of the lower animals. This is true. But to man alone has He given the ability to give meaning to those vibrations, primarily in language and in music. Spend the next few months really relishing sounds, enjoying all of the variations God has given to us and the meaningfulness of those variations. And as you do, thank Him for His gift of hearing.

Thanks to God for **those other three senses**

What a dull world it would be if we could only see and hear but could not taste and smell and touch the world around us. Thank God that food tastes good! Imagine what it would be like to have to eat bad-tasting food, or food which had no taste at all. And flowers wouldn't be half as good if they looked pretty but didn't have a smell.

The sense of touch introduces us to one of God's most beautiful gifts—sex. Sex has been so abused in our society that sometimes Christians have almost forgotten that it was God who "invented" it. Of all people, we have no reason to be in any way ashamed of sex. It's very likely, however, that you have never heard anyone in a church prayer meeting say a thanks to God for that wonderful gift. You be the first one to do it—next Wednesday night, seven P.M.! Or, if you are a little less bold, certainly say a thanks to God for the wonderful sense of touch which expresses itself in many ways.

In the pages that follow write your experiences in which God has taught you to be thankful for those three senses: taste, smell and touch.

Thanks to God for **the gift of a tongue**

If there is one part of the body whose power has been underestimated, it is probably the tongue. The Apostle James describes it as an instrument which, though small in size, can do great good or great evil. Like the rudder on a large ship, how we use the tongue determines the course of our life. James makes the striking statement, "No human being can tame the tongue" (3:8).

Despite these very real dangers of using the tongue to hurt others and ourselves, the tongue is one of the most glorious gifts God has given to man. Spend a few minutes imagining that everyone had no use of the tongue. The telephone, radio, even television would become useless. Even preaching would no longer be possible. In daily life you could not carry a simple conversation, or even sing a song. Try going without the use of the tongue for a single day. Then when you open your mouth again say a prayer aloud to God for the beautiful use of this voice and tongue. In the following pages write those experiences which come to you which make you appreciate fully the use of this little instrument, the tongue.

Thanks to God for **making my one unique body**

How very difficult it is for many of us to accept the particular body God has given us. Many of us find ourselves constantly comparing our own features to those of others, usually envying them and failing to appreciate the advantages of our own uniqueness. This is particularly true in America, where we have been subjected to a steady diet of anxiety-producing advertisements which often purposely attempt to make us reject the way we look in order to sell a product which might "help." Not that I am opposed to cosmetics—I use them myself—but the only "foundation make-up" that I have found to *work* is self-acceptance. When you can accept the body and face that God has given you, it's fun to play around with looking different. But when you *can't* accept yourself as you are, it's a hellish burden that never ends until that funeral director fixes your face and combs your hair for the last time.

I want it to be understood that I am in no way trying to offer an excuse for gluttony or the neglecting of personal hygiene. God will still love us even if we are overweight or need a bath, but He's very likely to want to give us a bar of soap and put a lock on the refrigerator. One of the reasons that some of us have a difficult time in thanking God for our body may well be the fact that it is no longer the same body that He gave to us. If we have neglected our health or abused our body, then we need to start by thanking God for the body that we once had. Maybe when we begin to do that, He might begin as well to help us—as we help *ourselves*—to rediscover the real person we were meant to be.

In the pages that follow, write about your own body-image, problems you may have had with it, and tell what God does for you to help you accept and love that one unique person who is you.

Thanks to God for **material blessings**

A few months ago my husband and I were in India. Never had either of us seen such desperate poverty. When we returned to the United States it seemed to us as though our old neighborhood had somehow been transformed into a country club setting for millionaires! We marveled at having sidewalks, sprinkler systems watering green lawns, chimneys which signified brick fireplaces, street lights and telephone wires overhead—a hundred material blessings that we had taken for granted before we left on our trip. Entering our house again we were absolutely staggered at the wealth which surrounded us—an electric refrigerator, our own fresh water system complete with hot as well as cold water, carpeting on the floors, screens on all the windows and a garage just for the housing of our automobile! We must be millionaires, we thought to ourselves, because we own two dogs and can feed them both! The local supermarket became to us now an absolute marvel to behold. After six months traveling in several underdeveloped countries, it took us two months before we took our first drink of American water without questioning first whether it was safe. God had really opened our eyes through this trip and we could now see and appreciate what we had previously simply taken for granted.

We are fully aware, of course, that there are many even here in America who are finding it difficult to make financial ends meet. But what we learned through that trip was that it is not the amount of material blessings a person has which makes him happy, but rather his appreciation of those that he does have. We had discovered many people who lived on the brink of poverty who were nevertheless happy with only a few of the possessions that most Americans can claim. One reason I think many people—many Christians, too—become "hooked" on possessions is that they fail to appreciate the possessions they already have.

On the pages that follow take the time to count your many material blessings. Ask God to teach you to be appreciative for what you do have, and patient with what you are perhaps missing. As He does, thank Him for each material possession of which you become appreciative.

Thanks to God for
things I take for granted

Every now and then, and especially while you are writing in this book, you will find yourself suddenly aware of something to be thankful for that you have completely taken for granted before. It will be a surprise to you, something that has been there right in front of your eyes but has never been appreciated. The list of such things could go on forever because we are indeed—all of us—mostly unaware of what God has done for us.

In the pages that follow write the experience of discovery—those moments in which you find something new to be thankful for which you have taken for granted before.

Thanks to God for **"bad experiences"**

Bad experiences—major life problems, tragic circumstances, or painful trials—have often destroyed what had *seemed* to be a strong faith in God. In fact, those whose faith is based on the experiences which happen to them are certainly destined to lose that faith, because very certainly some misfortune will strike them. God has never promised us a rose garden. Instead He has promised us that "in this world *ye shall* have tribulation." Unless we live in some kind of emotional Disneyland, troubles and tribulations will come our way, and if we—like Job's friends—believe that the righteous shall not suffer, then we are surely to be faced eventually with having to blame God or ourselves.

There is another kind of "emotional Disneyland" into which some Christians have retreated. Following the publication of Frances Hunter's excellent book *Praise The Lord Anyway,* there has arisen a large group of Christians who have misused her sound biblical advice. Sincere and heartfelt praise to God has become reduced to cute cliches casually quoted in the face of real tragedy. "Well, P.T.L.A.!" say such Christians to a family whose child has been killed by a drunken driver. Misunderstanding entirely what Mrs. Hunter was trying to say, they may feel that they are proving their faith in the Lord by mouthing such irresponsible cliches. It has been my observation that what they are really doing is trying to reassure themselves because they lack a deep faith in the Lord's providence, and so must try to turn real pain and trouble into just some new play in God's game strategy. My husband refers to this as a form of "Christian schizophrenia," which is a "faith" that maintains itself by means of a fantasy world which is out of contact with the *real* world of real pain, real suffering, real evil, and a real cross. Jesus didn't sweat blood in the Garden of Gethsemane because He lacked faith, but because He understood and faced the reality and pain of the cross He had to bear. Likewise we too experience pain and trial not so that we can simply learn to ignore it, or gloss over it with a quick P.T.L. irresponsibly mouthed, but by going through that pain and learning from it. In the next few pages write about those times when God has lead you through a "bad experience" and taught you to trust Him even more in going through it.

Thanks to God for **leading us not into temptation**

Recently I heard a young Christian describing how God had "tempted him" to fall back into drug addiction so as to show His power by rescuing him from these drugs. It's a dramatic story, and I'm glad that he was indeed rescued, but I doubt the correctness of his theological interpretation. God never leads us into temptation, in the sense of planning for us to get into temptation. God leads us, and temptations come along the path on their own. More often we stumble off the road to find a few temptations ourselves. Moreover, as Scripture tells us, every temptation is of a common form experienced by all other Christians as well. In other words, we can never claim that we had to face a "special" temptation that was more difficult to overcome. Besides that, God also makes it clear that He will always allow us a way to escape *any* temptation if it comes to a place where we are no longer able to bear it (1 Cor. 10:13).

In the pages that follow write about your experiences with temptations and thank God for the way which He found for you to be delivered from them. The story may be useful to someone else who reads of your own escape—or maybe to you yourself at a later time when that same temptation, or another one, faces you again.

Thanks to God for **lessons in living**

What has God taught you about living? Probably so many things that it will seem impossible to describe them here in a few pages. Patience, humility, the meaning of love, understanding of other people, gratitude, courage—the life lessons that the Lord attempts to teach each one of us are innumerable and the lessons continue for our entire lifetime. In the pages that follow write those most important lessons that you have learned. Tell how God taught it to you in each particular case, and thank Him for what He has done.

Thanks to God for **joy**

When the Apostle Paul lists the "fruit of the Spirit"—the results of the Holy Spirit's work in us—the first fruit mentioned is *joy*.

If God hasn't taught you to be joyful, it's probably still number one on His list, even if you don't think it's very important. You can go around with a long and serious, "dedicated" look on your face if you want to, but God would rather have you become just plain happy—*joyful*—before He has you become a biblical scholar or an evangelist. If you've become a scholar, soul-winner, or even "sanctified saint" without becoming joyful as well, you're not producing the first kind of fruit God's interested in.

Write about those experiences in which you *have* experienced joy (or maybe just good, wholesome "fun"). Thank God for all of the surface fun *and* deep joy which He has given.

Thanks to God for **answered prayers**

Personally, I think the greatest miracle God ever performs is the answers He gives to our individual prayers. That God should create the universe is a miracle, but what you would not expect is that the Creator of the universe would concern Himself to listen and reply to the very small and often "trivial" requests made of Him day by day by human individuals. No matter how unimportant we may be in the world's eyes or how minor our prayer may seem in the consequences of this world, it is never a trivial or unimportant matter to God.

And He never leaves one unanswered. As someone has said, "God *always* answers our prayers, often with a 'yes,' sometimes with a 'no,' sometimes with 'later,' but never with a 'maybe' or a 'don't bother me.' " In the pages that follow write the experiences you have had in which God has answered your prayers, and thank Him for answering them.

Thanks to God for **letting me question him**

One of my own favorite verses in the Bible is the answer given by the man to whom Jesus directed the question "Do you believe?"

"Yes, Lord, I believe; help my unbelief!" the man replied with complete honesty (Mark 9:24). Such is the attitude of the sincere questioner. The man wanted to have faith, and he did have *some* faith, but he needed more understanding. How very relaxing it is to see that Jesus did not reject him. How unlike Jesus are all too many of today's Christian leaders, as well as followers. Sometimes it seems that they have forgotten that the God we each seek to understand is the Creator of the immense universe in which we live. He is not likely to be surprised if we don't understand Him fully or if we have questions. Usually you will find that honest questions patiently asked will suddenly and unexpectedly be answered with understanding. In the pages that follow write about those experiences in which God has allowed you to question Him and has given you an answer, or has allowed you to continue questioning with peace of mind.

Thanks to God for **loving doubters too**

We have all read the story of "Doubting Thomas," to whom the Lord showed the nail prints in His hands and feet. Unfortunately, most sermons I have heard on the story of Doubting Thomas emphasized the dangers of doubting and the blessedness of belief. All that is so. But what is easily overlooked is the simple fact that Jesus loved Thomas even while he was doubting. Perhaps the most dangerous thought a Christian can have is that there is something that he can do which will make God stop loving him. Many of us feel that when we doubt, or sin, God withdraws His love from us. Such an idea is not only untrue, but its real danger is that it makes it about ten times harder for us to come back to the Father who has been grieving and waiting for our return all along.

Jesus told the story of the Prodigal Son in order to show us how much the Father loves us, even while we choose to doubt or turn from His love. Maybe you have experienced yourself what the Prodigal Son experienced. Think what it would be like if we did indeed have to prove ourselves, over and over again, to a father who didn't really love us. On the pages that follow, describe those moments when you have learned the beautiful feeling of being loved even in the midst of doubt.

Thanks to God for **promises that never fail**

The Bible is full of promises, unconditional guarantees from the Creator of the universe Himself. I was tempted to list them here, but instead I decided to let God teach them to you individually as you discover them individually in the Scriptures. When you discover one, write it on the following pages. When you discover a fulfilling of that particular promise in the details of your daily life, write also that experience. Slowly you will acquire a personal record of the faithfulness of our God who keeps His promises.

Thanks to God for the bible

Have you ever wondered what life would be like if God had not inspired the writing of the Bible? Considering the fact that there are probably a hundred cults deviating from the Bible itself, we would probably have to contend with a good ten thousand if there were no Bible at all! Any and every opinion concerning the existence and personality of God would be equally open for contention. How many times have you found comfort within the pages of the Bible? Or guidance?

In the pages that follow thank God for His Work. Specifically tell those experiences in which the Bible has been a very special blessing in your own life.

Thanks to God for **the voice of the holy spirit**

Before he left His disciples, Jesus told them, "It is to your advantage that I go away . . . if I go, I will send him [the Counselor, the Holy Spirit] to you" (John 16:7). Christians have very often failed to understand the meaning of this particular passage. Sometimes they tell themselves that "things would be a lot easier" if they were living in the time of Jesus. But Jesus said it was good that He leave us, because the Holy Spirit's presence would be in some way better. That's right! Even though the disciples were able to converse and see Jesus Himself—and how I would have liked to have been there myself, too—they had to be in His physical presence to talk to Him or to hear Him talk to them. But once the Holy Spirit came into the world, we are never alone; we are never without a voice from God!

In the pages that follow write about those experiences in which God's Holy Spirit has spoken clearly to you, directing your path or leading you in a very obvious way.

Thanks to God for **rules to protect me**

Modern man is afraid of rules. He may be so tied up in conformity that he's afraid to walk down the street without being sure that he's met the clothing, grooming, and general "cool behavior" rules of his peer society. But try to lay a rule on his head and he rebels as though you had threatened him with a life sentence in jail.

"Modern" Christians are all too often no different. They are ready to "sell all they have and follow Jesus," so long as they experience some kind of miraculous, personal call to service. But impose a rule, a boring, old-fashioned, noncharismatic law written (quite impersonally) for *everyone* to follow, and they somehow see it as a "legalistic trap," or just don't see it at all.

Rules are so friendly though. Without those wonderful rules that prescribe who should stop (red light) and who can keep on going (green light), it would be difficult to cross town at more than eight m.p.h. What a helpful "imposed standard of conduct"!

God wants to speed us along our way in the same fashion. Unfortunately, too many of His vehicle operators seem to have flunked their driving test, if not the written part, at least the driving part. Luckily, however, He never seems to tire of conducting traffic school for those who want to attend.

What has God taught you about the helpfulness of His laws? Write about the times when He's had to pull you over to the curb and give you a warning, or maybe a ticket. Have you thanked Him for that? Write about each new lesson as it happens to you.

Thanks to God for **things I forgot to thank him for**

Have you ever had to send a belated birthday card? It's always embarrassing for the sender, but as a sometimes receiver I can say for myself at least it's better to receive a belated card than none at all! I think God must feel the same way. It no doubt delights Him to receive every thank-you card on time, and now and then a few dozen roses of praise as well, but I think He is still very pleased to receive even those belated cards that we suddenly remember to send a few days, weeks, or even years later.

These pages are reserved for those belated thank-yous that you may now and then remember that you forgot to send.

Thanks to God for **just being himself**

Sometimes it seems that everybody wants something from God. I wonder what percentage of the prayers that reach heaven every day are asking for something. There is nothing wrong with that of course, but I wonder if God doesn't get "lonely" sometimes to talk to people who have nothing in mind but just being with Him, person to person. We all know how good it feels to talk with someone who is not trying to prove anything, who is relaxed about himself, and just enjoys being with you fully. Well, God must Himself be a million times more relaxed—and relaxing—to talk with. Certainly that ought to be part of our "praise" and "thankfulness," the experience of just being with God and experiencing Him as Himself.

In the following pages write about those times in which you have done just that—times when you had nothing to ask for and it seemed as though God had nothing to teach you, but you just enjoyed each other Person to person.

Afterword

The Apostle John closes his Gospel with the following words:

> But there are also many other things which Jesus did; were every one of them to be written, I suppose that the world itself could not contain the books that would be written. (21:25)

That statement is not only true of what Jesus did while He was on earth, but it is also true of the countless things He has done in each of our individual lives since then.

The Psalmist tells us "O taste and see that the Lord is good! Happy is the man who takes refuge in him" (Ps. 34:8). What you have recorded in this book is just a "taste" of the banquet the Lord has prepared for us. Use the following pages for recording some "extra desserts" that He offers to you. I think you'll soon discover that it's impossible to keep up with the One who makes our cups "runneth over."